Let's Explore India

by Walt K. Moon

BUMBA BOOKS™

LERNER PUBLICATIONS ◆ MINNEAPOLIS

Note to Educators:

Throughout this book, you'll find critical thinking questions. These can be used to engage young readers in thinking critically about the topic and in using the text and photos to do so.

Lerner Publications Company
A division of Lerner Publishing Group, Inc.
241 First Avenue North
Minneapolis, MN 55401 USA

For reading levels and more information, look up this title at www.lernerbooks.com.

Library of Congress Cataloging-in-Publication Data

Names: Moon, Walt K., author.
Title: Let's explore India / by Walt K. Moon.
Description: Minneapolis : Lerner Publications, [2016] | Includes bibliographical references and index. | Audience: Grades K–3.
Identifiers: LCCN 2016018691 (print) | LCCN 2016019481 (ebook) | ISBN 9781512430066 (lb : alk. paper) | ISBN 9781512430172 (pb : alk. paper) | ISBN 9781512430189 (eb pdf)
Subjects: LCSH: India—Juvenile literature.
Classification: LCC DS407 .M64 2016 (print) | LCC DS407 (ebook) | DDC 954—dc23

LC record available at https://lccn.loc.gov/2016018691

Manufactured in the United States of America
1 – VP – 12/31/16

Expand learning beyond the printed book. Download free, complementary educational resources for this book from our website, www.lerneresource.com.

Table of Contents

A Visit to India

India is in Asia.

Many people live

in India.

It is a large country.

India has huge mountains

in the north.

Other areas have wide plains.

Great rivers flow through India.

Wild elephants roam

on grasslands.

Crocodiles swim in rivers.

Tigers live in forests.

9

Teak forests grow in rainy areas.

Teak tree wood is strong.

People use it to build things.

What might people build with teak wood?

India has huge cities.

These cities have lots

of people.

But most Indians live

in small towns.

India has a long history.

This temple is more than a

thousand years old.

People come from far away

to see it.

Why might people visit an old temple?

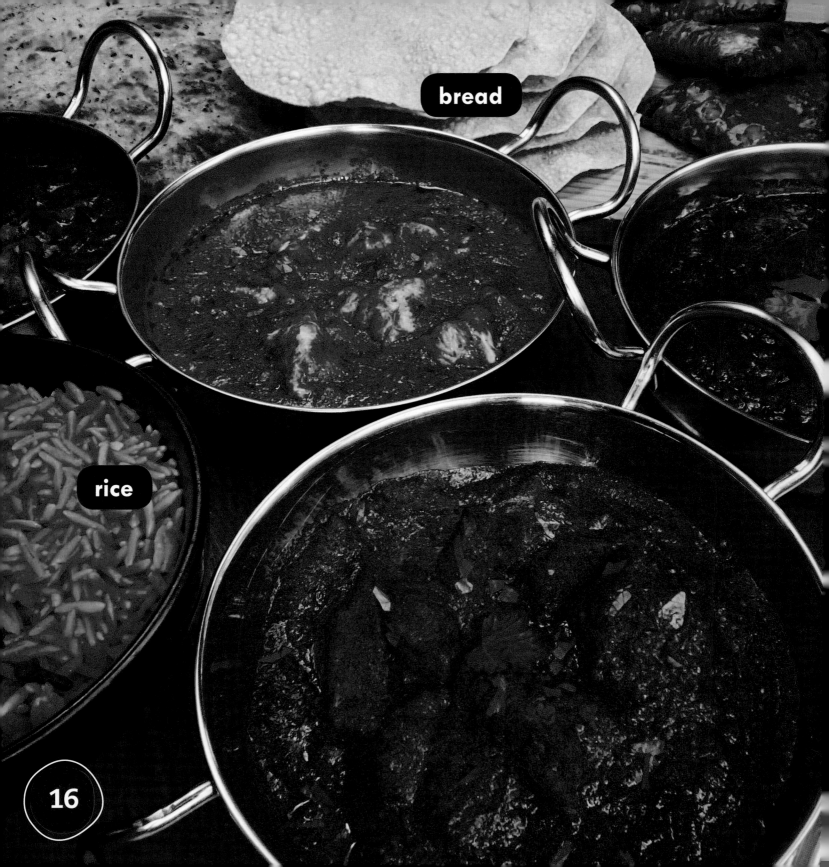

bread

rice

16

Indian food uses rice and bread.

People eat vegetables, chicken,

and lamb.

Sauces and spices add flavor.

Cricket is a major sport.

It is a bit like baseball.

Many Indians play

or watch it.

Can you see anything that cricket and baseball have in common?

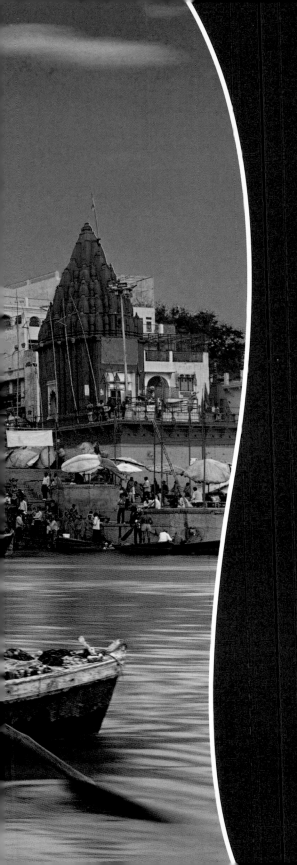

India is a

beautiful country.

There are many

things to see.

Would you like

to visit India?

21

Map of India

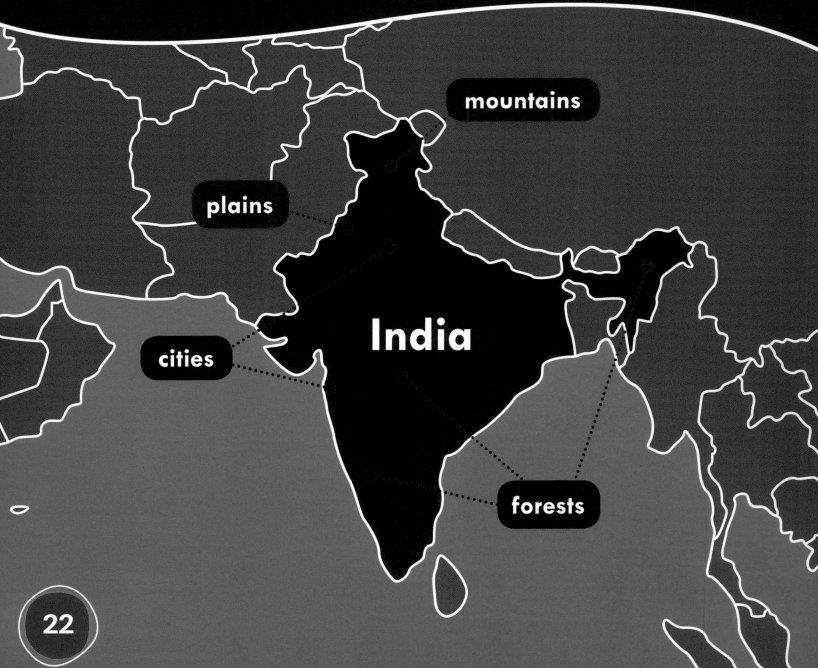

mountains

plains

cities

India

forests

Picture Glossary

cricket

a sport played with a bat and a ball

plains

big, flat pieces of land

teak

a kind of tree with hard wood and small white flowers

temple

a building used to honor a god

23

Index

Read More

Perkins, Chloe. *Living in . . . India.* New York: Simon & Schuster, 2016.

Raum, Elizabeth. *Taj Mahal.* Mankato, MN: Amicus, 2015.

Thomson, Ruth. *India.* New York: PowerKids Press, 2011.

Photo Credits

The images in this book are used with the permission of: © Karves/Shutterstock.com, pp. 4–5; © Andrey Armyagov/Shutterstock.com, p. 6; © Honey Cloverz/Shutterstock.com, pp. 8–9; © Peangdao/Shutterstock.com, p. 11; © Radiokafka/Shutterstock.com, pp. 12–13; © Pikoso.kz/Shutterstock.com, p. 15; © stocksolutions/Shutterstock.com, p. 16; © Stefano Ember/Shutterstock.com, pp. 18–19; © Lena Serditova/Shutterstock.com, pp. 20–21; © Red Line Editorial, p. 22; © SNEHIT/Shutterstock.com, p. 23 (top right).

Front Cover: © Olena Tur/Shutterstock.com.